TIME FOR KIDS READERS

International SPACE STATION

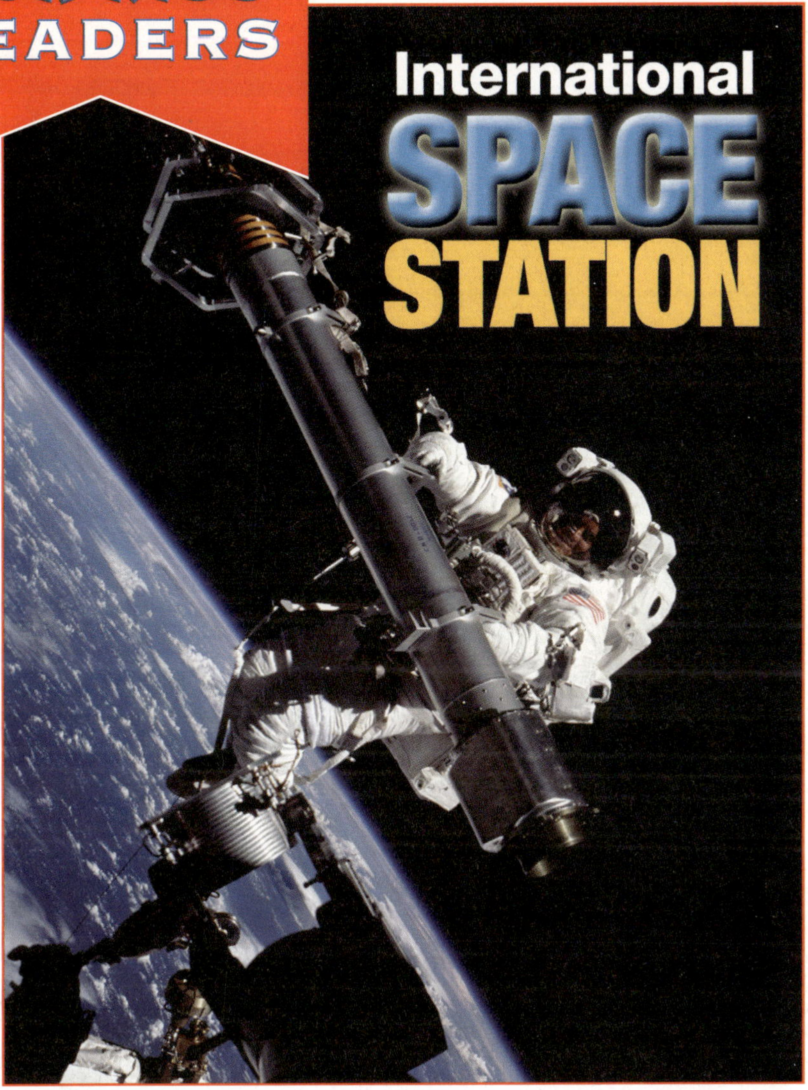

by Susan Ring

Harcourt

Orlando Austin Chicago New York Toronto London San Diego

Visit *The Learning Site!*
www.harcourtschool.com

What do you think it would be like to live and work in space? As you read this, there are people doing that. They are on board the International Space Station.

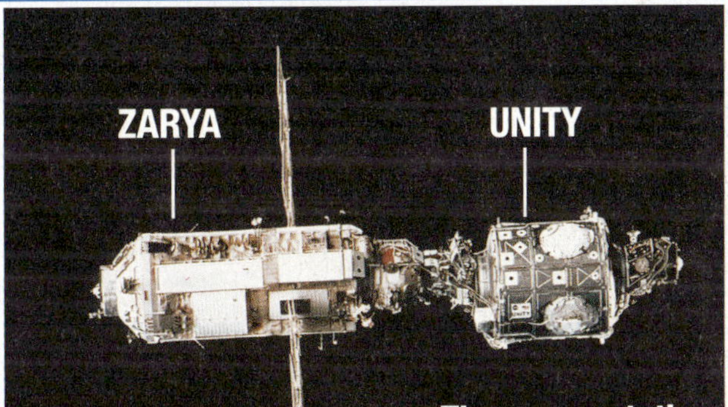

The space station started with these two parts.

The space station began with only two parts. One was from Russia. It was called *Zarya*, meaning "sunrise." The other part, from the United States, was called *Unity*.

100

Now the space station is about the weight of 100 elephants. When completed it will weigh close to one million pounds and will be made up of many parts.

1 International Space Station

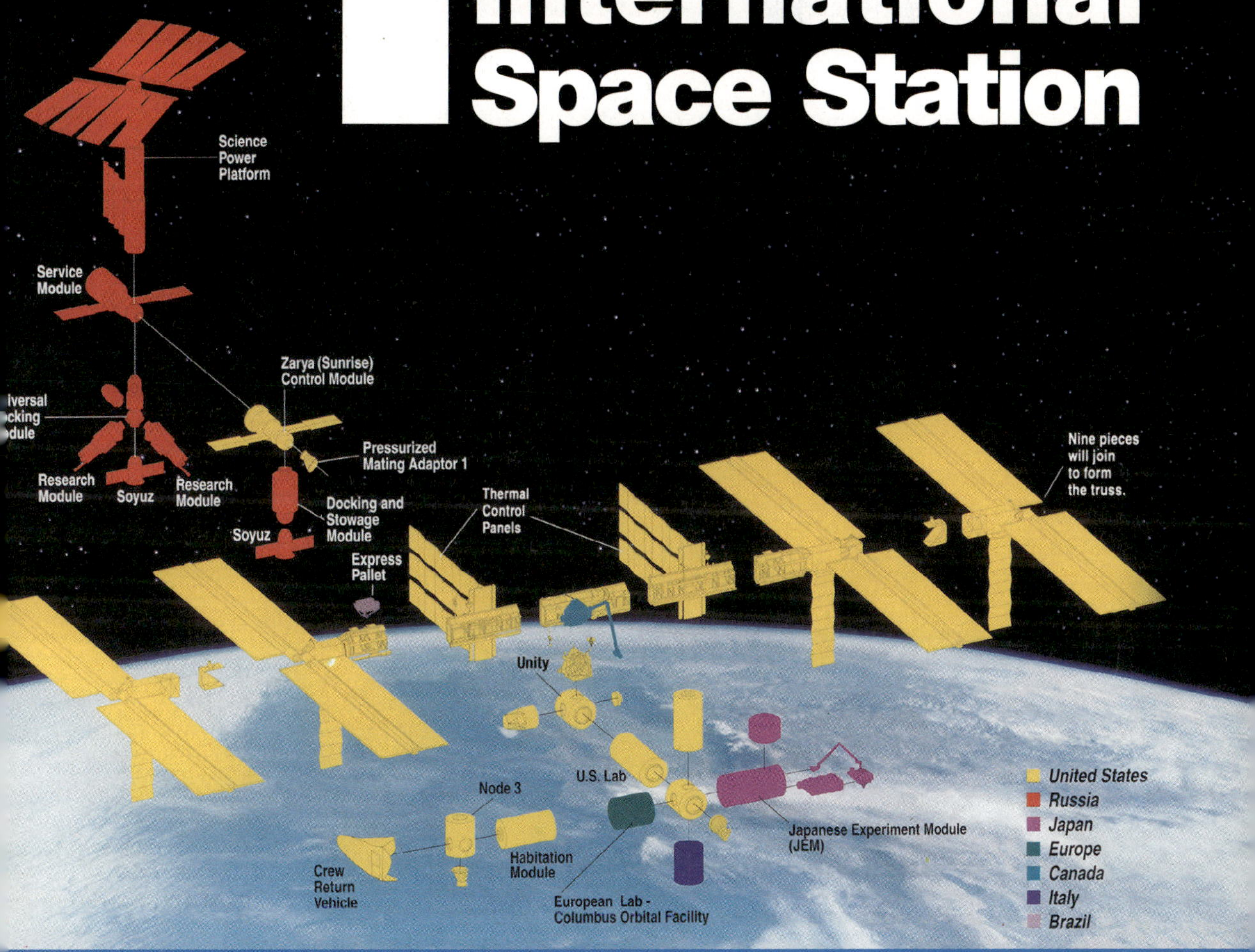

The main part is called the *truss*. All other parts connect to this long piece. Each section is made on Earth and sent up in rockets.

How are the parts put together? Astronauts go on spacewalks to work outside the space station. They are tied to it so they won't float off. Their tools are also tied in place.

An astronaut works in space. He is tied to an arm of the space station.

The International Space Station was made so astronauts could stay in space for a long time. Men and women from different countries live there and conduct experiments. Every day the astronauts hope to discover new things.

Canada

MF43H
CMX SACCO

An astronaut performs an experiment.

The space station will have six science labs. Many lab drawers are filled with experiments. The drawers can be taken out and sent back to Earth on a shuttle. A shuttle can also send up items the astronauts might need.

The astronauts have discovered that they can grow nearly perfect crystals in space. They are also mixing different kinds of metals. The metals become stronger than those on Earth. The astronauts hope to find out how and why that happens.

OVHD
HATCH
EXIT
PORT

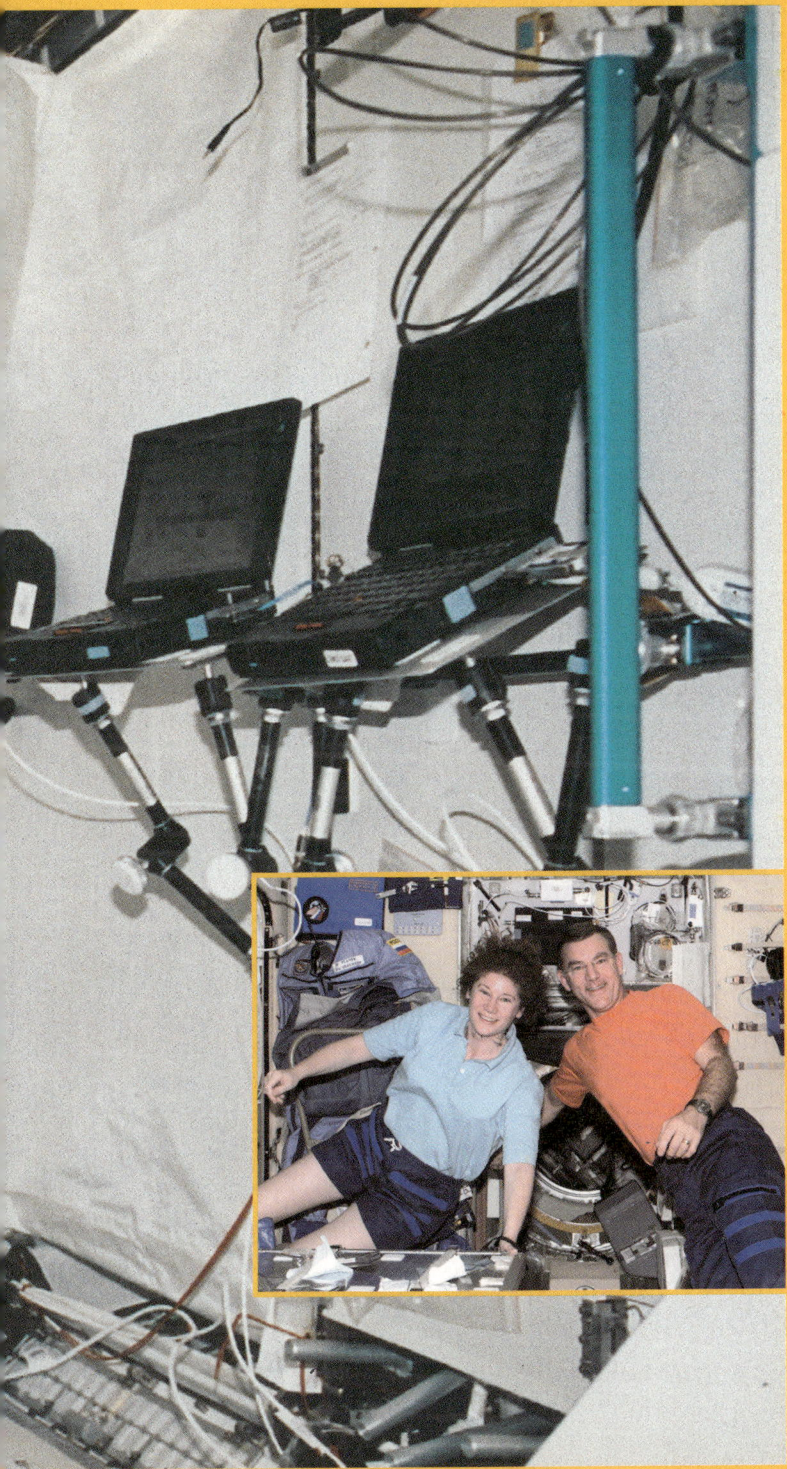

Astronauts want to know more about living without gravity. The astronauts study their bones, muscles, and lungs. This will help people plan for longer stays or farther travel in space.

Inside the space station are places for astronauts to live and work. They don't have to wear space suits all the time. They can spend the day almost as if they were on Earth.

Without gravity, astronauts float around the space station.

In zero gravity, astronauts can sleep upside down.

There is a kitchen where the astronauts cook meals. There are bunks to sleep in. They can study at a desk, exercise in the gym, and take a hot shower.

Huge solar panels outside the space station take in sunlight. The sun's power is then made into electricity. That electricity runs the computers, lights, and everything else on board.

Solar panels outside the space station turn sunlight into energy.

This picture shows the stages that an X-38 goes through when it lands.

What if the astronauts need to get out quickly? They have the X-38. This small vehicle can carry people back to Earth.

Perhaps the space station will one day send a spacecraft to Mars or to the moon. The spacecraft would have a shorter distance to travel than if it left from Earth. It could be bigger and heavier, and it would use less fuel.

The International Space Station is still growing. Maybe one day you'll go there. Then you will see for yourself what it is like to live in space.

Astronauts keep adding parts to the space station.